A Cook's Tour of DUBLIN

by Gillian Berwick

Foreword

1988 was the year of the Dublin Millenium. It was also the year in which Australians commemorated the arrival of the First Fleet.

Two hundred years ago many Irish people went to Australia unwillingly, hating to leave their homeland. Today young Irish people are flocking there looking upon it as a sort of promised land.

It is something of a paradox that a young Irish-Australian should reverse the procedure, and in this Millennial/Bicentennial year write a book about Dublin. Gillian is able then to view Ireland from something of the viewpoint of the homecoming stranger, able to see and savour many things that we overlook or take for granted.

Having been brought up in Australia, it is not surprising that she found a fascination in all that is old and traditional.

In Ireland we would probably concede that our basic ingredients such as salmon, beef, lamb, pork, poultry and cream (to say nothing of our whiskey, liqueurs and stout!) are of a very high quality. It is doubtful, however, if we would consider our country to rate highly in the world of haute cuisine. In her first major cookbook, *"Recipes from Irish Country Houses"*, Gillian demonstrates that in fact we rate very highly indeed on both counts.

Now Gillian has turned her attention to Dublin to catch something of its history and its character. This is neither a tourist guide to Dublin nor a history of Dublin but rather an experience of it by someone who is 'sympathetic' to its spirit and character, while at the same time being neither resident nor stranger.

Rita Corrie

Acknowledgements

First published in 1988 by Berwick Publishers.

Printed by Blacks of Cavan, Ireland.

Copyright
ISBN 0 9511612 2 9.

Editors: Rita Corrie, Mary Bond.

Photographer: Declan Corrigan.

By the same author –
"Making your Own Chocolates".
"Recipes from Irish Country Houses".

Introduction

Seeing Dublin in the serenity of a very early spring morning with the sombre mist not quite gone, the rising sun casting shafts of light onto the Victorian and Georgian façades you see the awakening of one of Europe's most colourful cities. Seagulls are there scavenging along the Quays of the River Liffey, oblivious to the 1000 years of the city's past. Although a bit tarnished here and there, Dublin is still capable of attracting thousands of tourists each year and sending them home enraptured with memories.

Enough history lies within the archives of literally dozens of Dublin's buildings to exhaust even the most avid historian, but a day spent just wandering the streets and meeting Dubliners can produce unexpected rewards.

The city centre itself is quite small and easy enough to explore on foot. Remains of the past are not difficult to find: there is Wood Quay, site of the Viking settlement dating from the 9th century A.D. and the Corn-market of medieval times. Present day Dublin, modern and vibrant is of course Grafton Street and its shopping arcades. Your tour of the past and present can provide you with a captivating glance or an absolutely exhausting marathon, depending on what you want to make of it.

Outside Trinity College are statues of Goldsmith and Burke representing the opulence of the city's culture. Find St. Stephen's Green – one of the many pleasant squares where one can sit in the parkland – an oasis in the centre of a teeming, bustling city.

I mention St. Stephen's Green because its attractive streets and alleyways abound with world class restaurants and cafés. This is what "A Cook's Tour of Dublin" is all about.

The city is a late-to-bed (and not an early riser) one. As soon as the shops close the city becomes alive with Dubliners and visitors alike. The more sophisticated head for the truly splendid restaurants and the gay, noisy youth parade gravitates towards the cafés, pubs, bistros and "take aways".

Dublin is the capital of a country which produces food of a very high standard and chefs who are used to only the best. If you feel virtuous after a day of cultural digestion (or indigestion as the case may be) now is the time to be pampered by the city's great chefs.

Gillian Berwick,
Emo Court,
Emo, Co. Laois

CONVERSIONS

Hints on Measurements:

One wonders why we have to complicate our lives by becoming "metricated". All our old and favorite recipes are in pounds, ounces and sometimes even in handfuls! The shops continue to sell in pounds in some cases and kilograms in others, while oranges are sold in units and eggs in dozens. The secret is not to *worry*, usually close proximity in measurements doesn't spell disaster, but do use the same measurement throughout the recipe, i.e. metric, imperial or cups.

For my American readers, here are a few points:
Unless otherwise stated level spoons and cup measurements should be used.
1 lb is actually 454 grams.
Bread Soda is the same as Baking Soda and Bicarbonate of Soda.
Cornflour is the same as Cornstarch.
Treacle is the same as Molasses.
Capsicums are the same as Peppers.

Contents

History

9. Churches.
13. Guinness's Brewery.
23. The Mansion House.
27. Dublin's Great Georgian Squares.
35. Gandon's Dublin.
41. The Royal Hospital, Kilmainham.
45. Trinity College.
51. History of Dublin.
57. Leinster House.
63. The National Gallery.
67. Dublin Castle.
71. The Whiskey Corner.
73. The Rotunda Hospital.
75. The Shelbourne Hotel.
77. St. Stephen's Green.
79. The University Church.
81. Modern Dublin.

Recipes

6. Dips n' Dunks.
11. Soups.
15. Breads, Muffins and Butters.
25. Salads.
29. Fish.
37. Main Courses.
43. Vegetables.
47. Desserts.
53. Fruit Salads.
59. Cakes.
65. Jams and Preserves.
69. Irish Coffee.
85. Index.

DIPS N' DUNKS

Fruit and Nut Dip

225 grams/8 oz/1 cup
cream cheese
(softened).
110 grams/4 oz/½ cup
pineapple crushed and
drained.
1½ tspns garlic salt.

1 tblspn chopped parsley.
1 tblspn diced green
capsicums.
1 tblspn grated onion.
55 grams/2 oz/½ cup
walnuts, crushed.

Mix together the cream cheese, pineapple, garlic salt, parsley, capsicum, onion and only half the walnuts.
Place in serving dish and decorate with remaining walnuts. Chill before serving.
Serve with water biscuits.
This freezes well if you wish to make it in quantity.

Apricot and Cottage Cheese Dip

6 dried apricots.
120 ml/4 fl oz/½ cup
orange juice.
225 grams/8 oz cottage
cheese.

1 dessertspn chives,
chopped.
120 ml/4 fl oz/½ cup
cream.

Simmer the dried apricots and orange juice over a medium heat for about five minutes. Set aside to cool. Combine the cottage cheese and chives and mix the cream through. Lastly dice the apricots and add to the cheese mixture. Refrigerate before serving.

BIRTHPLACE OF

WILLIAM BUTLER YEATS

POET · DRAMATIST · AUTHOR

JUNE 13 1865

Avocado Dip

2 large avocadoes.
3 hard boiled eggs, (mashed).
1 lemon, squeezed and grated.
1 clove garlic.
1 tspn chopped chives.
1 dessertspn chopped parsley.

60 ml/2 fl oz/¼ cup cream.
Salt and freshly ground pepper to taste.
Cayenne pepper, (optional).

Halve the avocadoes, remove stones. Put flesh into bowl and mash well. Add hard boiled eggs, lemon juice and rind, garlic, chives, parsley and cream. Add salt and pepper to taste. Mix well. Serve garnished with a dash of cayenne pepper, parsley and a slice of lemon. Use water biscuits or melba toast as an accompaniment.

Garden Dip

120ml/4 fl oz/½ cup sour cream.
60ml/2 fl oz/¼ cup mayonnaise.
1 dessertspn sugar.
½ tspn salt.
Freshly ground pepper.
¼ cup each of chopped spring onions, radish, chives and capsicum (green and red).

½ tspn horseradish sauce.
½ clove garlic, chopped fine.

In a food processor or blender mix together sour cream, mayonnaise, sugar, salt and pepper. Stir in chopped vegetables, horseradish and garlic.
Serve with carrot and celery sticks.

From left to right: Apricot and Cottage Cheese Dip, Avocado Dip, Cheese and Walnut Dip.

Churches of Dublin

Walking down Grafton Street it is easy to miss the little yellow sign on the lamp post pointing the way to Christ Church Cathedral, thus the opportunity to embark on an ethnic and ecclesiastical side-tour, quite as fascinating as Dorothy's sojourn down the yellow brick road. Wend your way past the Bank of Ireland, a beacon of the City's modern commercialism, up Dame Street, past Dublin Castle (which you must visit on another occasion) and you eventually arrive at a cluster of truly magnificent churches in an area of supreme historical importance.

On the present site of Christ Church (more correctly called Cathedral of the Holy Trinity) a wooden church was built in 1038 by Sitric, King of Dublin's Norsemen and Donat, first Bishop of Dublin. It was demolished in 1169 by the developers of the day and completely rebuilt by Richard de Clare of Pembroke ("Strongbow" to his friends). How nice to know that "developers" too have their place in history, and are not just a modern phenomenon – a product of the bulldozer era.

Since then there have been several additions and subtractions leaving Dublin with a beautiful panorama from the river bank. Below Christ Church are some of the last remaining remnants of the old city walls and the site of recently unearthed Viking relics – now sadly smothered by two concrete 20th century municipal office blocks. Nearby is St. Nicholas of Myra, – a little gem of a church both inside and out. Further back from the river is St. Patrick's Cathedral, an enormous church built in 1191, steeped in history and antiquity. Here is the site where St. Patrick is said to have baptised the citizens in the 5th century A.D. The site over the River Poddle on wet marshy ground, was an exceptionally bad one for such a massive Cathedral, but its religious significance made it a compelling choice.

Jonathan Swift was once Dean of St. Patrick's and wrote some of his greatest works including "Gulliver's Travels" during his tenure here. He is buried in the Cathedral – where that very Irish expression "chance your arm" originated. The Earl of Kildare, in pursuit of the Earl of Ormond, who had taken refuge in the Chapter House, cut a hole in one of the doors to grasp the hand of his enemy. Today, you can still see the door with the hole in it. This church is a fascinating museum of Irish history and culture. The Choir School, founded in 1432, educates boys for the famous choir and here they took part in the first ever public performance of Handel's Messiah in 1742, which was conducted by Handel himself in the Cathedral.

The area around these churches, the "Coombe", (a relic from the heyday of the Wool Trade) and the "Liberties" are almost tribal parts of Old Dublin. Very tight-knit communities have lived here for generations and are proud of their heritage and lineage. There are little alleyways and street names such as "Handkerchief Alley" and "Cow Parlour". If you get lost you might end up in Synge Street where George Bernard Shaw was born in 1856. If by now you are a little footsore but concious of a prevailing smell of brewing in the air you might be tempted to leave the ecclesiastical heights, follow your nose down to the River Liffey and head for Guinness!

"The Dean was famous in his time
And had a kind of knack for rhyme".
Jonathan Swift (1667-1745)

St. Patrick's Cathedral.

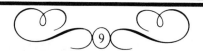

SOUPS

Cucumber Soup

1 large cucumber.
30 grams/1 oz/2 tblspns butter.
1 dessertspn diced spring onions.
20 grams/⅔ oz/2 tblspns flour.
900 ml/30 fl oz/3¾ cups chicken stock.
Salt and freshly ground pepper.
2 egg yolks.
60 ml/2 fl oz/¼ cup milk.
Chopped parsley to garnish.

Wash cucumber and cut into slices. Melt butter in a saucepan. Add the cucumber and spring onions and sauté over a gentle heat for 5-10 minutes or until cucumber is soft. Stir in the flour and cook for 1-2 minutes. Add the stock and simmer for 10 minutes. Blend in a liquidizer or food processor.

Add seasoning to taste. Beat the egg yolks, add the milk and some of the soup. Mix and return to soup. Heat but **do not allow to boil.** Garnish and serve.
SERVES 6.

Potato and Chervil Soup

30 grams/1 oz/2 tblspns butter.
450 grams/1 lb potatoes, peeled and sliced.
2 small onions, sliced.
900 ml/30 fl oz/3¾ cups stock.
1 bay leaf.
120 ml/4 fl oz/½ cup cream.
Salt and freshly ground pepper.
3 tblspns freshly chopped chervil.

Melt the butter, add potatoes and onions. Cook gently for 5-10 minutes, stirring frequently. Add the stock, and bay leaf. Simmer until potatoes are soft. Remove bay leaf. Blend the soup in a food processor. Return to saucepan. Stir in the cream and chervil. Season to taste. Reheat but do not boil.

SIR
JONAH BARRINGTON
1760 – 1834
MEMOIR WRITER

LIVED HERE

Onion Soup with White Wine

With the cheese and croûtons this soup is almost a meal by itself: alone, the soup is delicate and is ideal to serve before a heavy main course.

85 grams/3 oz/6 tblspns butter.
4 onions (diced finely).
¾ litre/24 fl oz/3 cups chicken stock.

250 ml/8 fl oz/1 cup white wine.
1 bay leaf.
Salt and freshly ground pepper to taste.

Optional:

Croûtons.
Grated cheese.

Chopped parsley and or chives to garnish.

Melt the butter in a saucepan. Add the diced onions and sauté until just soft. Add stock, white wine and bay leaf. Simmer for 15-25 minutes. Season to taste.

Optional. Serve into dishes and sprinkle on croûtons and cheese. Put under the grill to brown the cheese. Garnish.
SERVES 6.

Guinness

In a city where pubs shine like beacons on every street corner (and several places in between) Guinness is the national brew.

The Brewery was started by Arthur Guinness on the banks of the Liffey at St. James's Gate in 1759. For generations the Guinness barges transported their black ale down the river, to the port and onwards to all corners of the globe. Modern transport has replaced the colourful barges and horse drawn wagons, but Guinness still retains its pride of place as the world's leading stout. It has been used in cooking in Irish kitchens almost since its inception, particularly to enrich the traditional dark Irish fruit cake.

Today the Brewery is well worth a visit. As one of the world's leading breweries, and one of the oldest, it combines history, culture and interest and is a stepping stone through Dublin's past. Visitors are welcome – there is a little pub where you can rest your feet and Guinness takes care of the rest!

"And still they gazed and still the wonder grew, how one small head could carry all he knew."
Oliver Goldsmith, (1730-1774)

Entrance to Guinness Brewery.

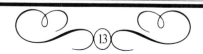

BREADS, MUFFINS & BUTTERS

Date & Bran Tea-Loaf

110 grams/4 oz/2 cups
   All Bran
285 grams/10 oz/2 cups
   flour.
55 grams/2oz/¼ cup
   sugar
1 tspn salt
2 tspns baking powder.
500 ml/16 fl oz/2 cups
   milk.

55 grams/2 oz/¼ cup
   butter, melted.
45 grams/1½ oz/⅔ cup
   coconut.
75 grams/ 2 oz/½ cup
   dates, finely chopped.
2 eggs.

Soak the All Bran in the milk and set aside.
Sift the dry ingredients together and add the
dates. Add the melted butter and eggs to the
All Bran mixture. Finally add the All Bran
mixture to the dry ingredients. Mix well so
as to incorporate the flour and put into a
greased loaf tin dusted with flour.
Bake at 180°C/350°F/Regulo 4 for 40 minutes
to 1 hour.

Aussie Damper

This bread originated from the Irish Soda
Bread. It was probably taken to Australia by
early Irish settlers. The original bread, made
from a simple flour and water dough, was
cooked in the oven or by winding the dough
around a stick and cooking it over the camp
fires in the Australian outback.
Today the recipe is improved by using self-
raising flour and adding butter and sugar.

570 grams/1¼ lb/5 cups
   self-raising flour.
Pinch salt.
1 dessertspn castor
   sugar.

55 grams/2 oz/¼ cup
   butter.
250-300 ml/8-10 fl oz/
   1-1¼ cups milk.
Beaten egg to glaze.

Sift the dry ingredients into a bowl. Rub in
the butter. Add enough milk to make a soft
dough and mix through. Turn out onto a
floured surface and knead lightly until dough
is smooth. Shape into a round, and place onto
a greased tray. Mark across into eight sections
and brush with beaten egg. Bake at 180°C/
350°F/Regulo 4 for 40-50 minutes or until
lightly browned and sounds hollow when
tapped underneath.
Serve hot.

Barmbrack

1.350 kgs/3 lb plain flour.
1 tspn mixed spice.
2 tspns salt.
900 ml/1½ pints/3¾ cups milk.
55 grams/2 oz yeast.
110 grams/4 oz/½ cup sugar.
110 grams/4 oz/½ cup butter or margarine

450 grams/1 lb/3 cups sultanas.
110 grams/4 oz/¾ cup currants and raisins mixed.
110 grams/4 oz/¾ cup mixed peel.

Grease and flour 2 round cake tins. Sieve together all dry ingredients except sugar and fruit. Mix the yeast with a tspn of the sugar and half the milk. Sprinkle a little flour on top and leave in a warm place for 10 minutes. Mix in the flour, add remaining liquid and mix thoroughly. Knead into a ball and turn onto a floured surface. Knead for 15 minutes or until the dough no longer feels sticky. Put into a greased bowl and leave to rise for ½ hour. Punch down and flatten to a large round. Place butter/margarine, sugar, and dried fruit in the middle and work in these ingredients by kneading until evenly incorporated in the dough. Return the dough to greased bowl, let rise for a further 30 minutes. Divide in half and shape so as to fit tins. Cover and leave to rise until dough reaches top of tins. Brush with milk and bake for about 50 minutes at 200°C/400°F/Regulo 6 or until hollow when tapped.

Shelbourne Hotel Brown Bread

1½ kilos/3 lb 6 oz wholemeal flour.
1 tspn salt.

2 tspns black treacle.
1½ litres/2½ pints water.
84 grams/3 oz fresh yeast.

Mix the flour and salt and warm. Mix the treacle and half the water well, and add the yeast. Place the water, treacle and yeast in a warm place for 5 minutes or until frothy on top.
Make a well in the flour and pour in the yeast mixture: mix with a wooden spoon and add the remainder of the water. When well mixed, the dough should be wettish.
Place the dough into 4 greased loaf tins, only half filling each. Place the tins in a warm place, covering with a damp cloth. Leave to rise for 20 minutes or until the bread has risen sufficiently (approximately doubled in size). Bake in a preheated oven at 220°C/420°F/Regulo 7 for 40-45 minutes. When cooked, the bread should be golden brown and sound hollow when tapped underneath.
Remove from tins and wrap in a damp cloth before serving.
Yield 4 loaves.

Irish Wholemeal Soda Bread

Ireland is the home of soda bread, made with either wholemeal or white flour. The traditional cross on the top is to let the devil out!

340 grams/12 oz/3 cups coarse ground wholemeal flour.
225 grams/8 oz/2 cups white self-raising flour.
1 tspn salt.

1 tspn bicarbonate of soda.
1 dessertspn sugar.
Approx. 300-470 ml/ 10-16 fl oz/1¼-2 cups buttermilk.

Sift together all the dry ingredients. Make a well in the centre and add enough buttermilk to produce a moist but firm dough. Turn onto a floured surface and knead lightly.
Form into a rounded shape and place on a floured baking sheet. Score a cross on the top. Brush with buttermilk. Bake at 200°C/400°F/Regulo 6 for about 40 minutes or until the bread sounds hollow when tapped underneath. Cool on a wire rack.

Variation. For Muesli Bread: replace half the wholemeal flour with muesli and proceed as above.

Herb Soda Bread

450 grams/1 lb/4 cups plain flour.
1¼ tspns baking soda.
1 tspn salt.
1-2 tblspns chopped parsley.

1½ tspns mixed herbs.
300-350 ml/10-12 fl oz/ 1¼-1½ cups buttermilk.

Sift together all dry ingredients. Add the herbs. Make a well in the centre and mix in enough buttermilk to make a soft but firm dough. Knead lightly and form into a rounded shape. Place on a floured baking sheet and mark a cross on top. Brush with buttermilk. Sprinkle with extra chopped parsley and mixed herbs.
Bake at a preheated 200°C/400°F/Regulo 6. for about 40 minutes or until the bread sounds hollow when tapped underneath. Cool on a wire rack.

THE ORMOND HOTEL
IS THE SETTING
FOR THE EPISODE
THE SIRENS
IN
JOYCES ULYSSES

Cornmeal Bread

If you haven't baked with yeast before don't be intimidated. This recipe is very easy and cornbread makes wonderful toast.

15 grams/½ oz yeast granules.	85 grams/3 oz/⅜ cup butter.
120 ml/4 fl oz/½ cup warm water.	2 tspns salt.
400 ml/14 fl oz/1¾ cups milk, scalded.	900 grams/2 lb/8 cups plain flour.
85 grams/3 oz/⅜ cup granulated sugar.	2 eggs, whisked.
	140 grams/5 oz/1 cup cornmeal.

Soften the yeast in the warm water. Set aside for 5-10 minutes or until frothy on top. Meanwhile, in a bowl, combine milk, sugar, butter and salt. Stir until the butter has melted. Cool until tepid. Add 285 grams/10 oz/2½ cups of the flour and beat until smooth. Add dissolved yeast, the whisked eggs, and cornmeal. Beat until smooth. Add enough of the remaining flour to make a soft dough. Turn out onto a floured surface and knead for 5-10 minutes or until the dough is no longer sticky. Put into an oiled bowl. Leave in a warm place, cover and let rise until it is double in size. This should take 1-2 hours. Punch down. Knead lightly and divide in half. Put into greased loaf tins and leave in a warm place to rise until double in size, about 1-2 hours.
Brush with milk, sprinkle with cornmeal and bake at 190°C/375°F/Regulo 5 for about 30-45 minutes or until brown and hollow when tapped on top.
Yield 2 loaves.

White Soda Bread

450 grams/1 lb/4 cups plain flour.	1 tspn salt.
1 tspn bicarbonate of soda.	1 tspn sugar.
	Approx 450 ml/15 fl oz/ 2 cups buttermilk.

Sift all dry ingredients together. Make a well in the centre and add enough buttermilk to make a moist but firm dough. Turn onto a floured surface and knead lightly for a few minutes. Shape into a round and place on a floured baking tin. Using a knife mark a cross on the top and brush with buttermilk. Bake at 200°C/400°F/Regulo 6 for about 40 minutes or until lightly browned and sounds hollow when tapped underneath. Cool on a wire rack.

Cornmeal Muffins

140 grams/5 oz/1 heaped cup flour.
2 tspns baking powder.
½ tspn baking soda.
¼ tspn salt.
55 grams/2 oz/¼ cup sugar.
140 grams/5 oz/1 cup cornmeal.
55 grams/2 oz/¼ cup butter, melted.
1 egg, beaten.
250 ml/8 fl oz/1 cup milk.

Preheat oven to 200°C/400°F/Regulo 6. Sift together dry ingredients and mix well. In a separate bowl combine the melted butter, milk and egg.
Add to the dry ingredients and mix only enough to incorporate. ⅔ fill oiled muffin tins. Sprinkle with extra cornmeal if desired. Bake for about 20-25 minutes or until well risen and firm. Remove from tins after 5 minutes.
Serve warm with butter.
Yield 12

Muesli Muffins

225 grams/8 oz/2 cups plain flour, sifted.
1½ tspns baking powder.
1 tspn baking soda.
¾ tspn salt.
55 grams/2 oz/scant ¼ cup brown sugar.
170 grams/6 oz/2 cups muesli.
110 grams/4 oz/½ cup butter, melted.
120 ml/4 fl oz/½ cup milk.
120 ml/4 fl oz/½ cup yoghurt.
2 eggs, beaten.
1 tspn vanilla essence.

Preheat oven to 200°C/400°F/Regulo 6. Sift together the flour, baking powder, soda, and salt. Add the brown sugar and muesli and mix well. In a separate bowl, combine the melted butter, milk, yoghurt, eggs and vanilla essence. Add this to the dry ingredients. Mix only enough to incorporate. ⅔ fill the oiled muffin tins. Bake for about 20-25 minutes or until well risen and golden. Remove from tins after 5 minutes. Serve warm with butter.
Yield 12.

BERNARD SHAW
AUTHOR OF MANY PLAYS
WAS
BORN IN THIS HOUSE
26 JULY 1856

Raspberry Muffins

225 grams/8 oz/2 cups plain flour.
2 tspns baking powder.
Pinch salt.
85 grams/3 oz/⅜ cup sugar.
110 grams/4 oz/½ cup butter, melted.

170 ml/6 fl oz/¾ cup milk.
1 egg, beaten.
½ cup fresh raspberries or tinned (well drained) (tossed in 30 grams/1 oz/¼ cup flour)

Preheat oven to 200°C/400°F/Regulo 6. Sift all dry ingredients into a bowl. Mix thoroughly. In a separate bowl, combine the melted butter, milk and egg. Add to the dry ingredients and mix only enough to incorporate. Toss raspberries in flour and fold into wet mixture. Spoon into oiled muffin tins until ¾ full and bake for 20-30 minutes or until done. Allow to remain in tins for a further 5 minutes so that they retain their shape.
Yield. 12.

Alternatively. Half fill the muffin pan with batter, add a teaspoon of the raspberries and then enough batter until ¾ full.

Orange Muffins

225 grams/8 oz/1¾ cups flour.
2½ tspns baking powder.
½ tspn salt.
55 grams/2 oz/¼ cup sugar.
55 grams/2 oz 1 cup mixed peel.

Grated rind and juice of 1 orange.
120 ml/4 fl oz/½ cup milk.
75ml/2½ fl oz/⅓ cup vegetable oil.
1 beaten egg.

Sift the dry ingredients together in a bowl. Add the peel. In a separate bowl beat together the egg, orange rind and juice, milk and vegetable oil. Add to dry ingredients and mix only enough to moisten the flour mixture.
¾ fill the greased muffin tins and bake at 200°C/400°F/Regulo 6 for fifteen to twenty minutes.
Serve warm with orange marmalade.

Tips on Muffin Making:

1. When combining the wet and dry ingredients, stir only enough to moisten. The batter should be lumpy.

2. Never serve a muffin cold!

SAVOURY BUTTERS

Grain Mustard Butter

110 grams/4 oz/½ cup
   unsalted butter,
   softened.
2 tspns Old Grain Style
   Mustard.

Few drops Tabasco
   sauce.

Mix the butter, mustard and Tabasco sauce together. Place in icing bag. Using a star shaped nozzle, pipe individual stars onto a tray lined with Bakewell paper. Refrigerate until needed.

Red Paprika Butter

110 grams/4 oz/½ cup
   butter, softened.

1 tspn ground paprika.
Dash cayenne.

Mix the butter, paprika and cayenne together. Put into a butter dish and refrigerate until needed.

Garlic Butter

110 grams/4 oz/½ cup
   butter, softened.
2 cloves garlic, crushed.
1 tspn lemon juice.

1 tspn lemon rind,
   (grated).
Salt and ground pepper if
   desired.

Mix the butter, garlic, lemon juice, rind and seasoning.
Put butter into a mould and refrigerate before serving or using for garlic bread.

Herb Butter

110 grams/4 oz/½ cup
   butter, softened.
1 tspn lemon juice.
1 tblspn chopped parsley

and chives, mixed.
3 tblspns other fresh
   mixed herbs, finely
   chopped.

Mix butter, lemon juice, half the parsley and chives and half the herbs. Shape into oblong and chill. Coat with remaining parsley, chives and herbs. Cut into 1¼ cm/½ inch pieces. Use as an accompaniment for meat and fish.

From left to right: Shelbourne Hotel Brown Bread, Aussie Damper, Irish Wholemeal Soda Bread, Barmbrack, White Soda Bread, Herb Bread, Cornmeal Bread, Savoury Butters.

The Mansion House

If you walk along St. Stephen's Green and turn into Dawson Street (which runs parallel to Grafton Street), you can't miss the Mansion House which looks like a charming grown-up doll's house. Set back from the road, it was built in 1710 by Joshua Dawson (after whom the street is named) for his own use. In 1714 it was chosen as the residence for the Lord Mayor. Before the building was completed it was sold to the corporation for a sum of £3,500. A rent of 40 shillings per year was also charged along with a six pound loaf of double-refined sugar at Christmas!

The plaster façade, the portico and the roundroom were 19th century additions and the City of Dublin boasted that it had a Mayoral palace before The City of London.

The City motto - "Obedientia Civium Urbis Felicitas" translated "The Obedience of the Citizens produces a happy City" – might come as a surprise to today's City's populace.

The Mansion House.

SALADS

Capsicum and Kiwifruit Salad

2 ripe tomatoes.
85 grams/3 oz yellow
    capsicum.
2 kiwifruit.
2 tblspns vegetable oil.
2 tspns white wine
    vinegar.
½ tspn Dijon mustard.

Honey.
Salt and pepper.
3 leaves of basil or a
    pinch of dried basil
    may be added to
    dressing 10 minutes
    before serving.

Slice tomato and capsicum. Peel and slice kiwifruit. Arrange decoratively in a small dish. Using a fork, whisk the oil, vinegar, mustard and enough honey to taste. Season and pour over.

SERVES 2.

Celery and Apple Salad

1 whole head celery.
½ melon.
3 firm, red apples.
55 grams/2 oz/½ cup
    walnuts.
Juice of ½ lemon.
Cos and endive lettuce
    leaves.
3 slices yellow capsicum.

2 olives.
110 grams/4 oz cottage
    cheese.
120 ml/4 fl oz/½ cup
    cream.
120 ml/4 fl oz/½ cup
    mayonnaise
Salt and freshly ground
    pepper.

Dice the celery and apple. Scoop the flesh out of the melon using a melon baller. Mix celery, fruits and walnuts together and pour the lemon juice over.

Arrange on a platter of lettuce leaves and garnish with capsicum and olives.

Lastly beat cream, mayonnaise and cottage cheese together. Season if required. Serve with the salad.

Coleslaw with Toasted Hazelnuts

½ medium size cabbage.
2 small onions.
2 stalks celery.
2 carrots.
225 grams/8 oz/1 cup
   pineapple, (optional).
170 ml/6 fl oz/¾ cup
   mayonnaise.

1 tblspn white wine
   vinegar.
Salt and freshly ground
   pepper.
Toasted hazelnuts

Finely shred the cabbage, onions and celery. Grate the carrots. Cut the pineapple into pieces. Mix together mayonnaise, vinegar and seasoning. Combine top five ingredients and mix through the mayonnaise mixture. Sprinkle toasted hazelnuts on top.

Cucumber in Sour Cream Sauce

1 small cucumber.

1 tspn salt.

Sauce

120 ml/4 fl oz/½ cup
   whipped sour cream.
1 tspn vinegar.

2 drops Tabasco sauce.
2 tblspns chopped chives.
½ tblspn chopped dill.

Slice the cucumber very thinly in a food processor or by hand. Sprinkle with salt and let stand for one hour. Drain and dry thoroughly. Combine sauce ingredients and pour over cucumber slices.

FAILTE DUBHLINN

DANIEL
O'CONNELL
(THE LIBERATOR)
1775 – 1847
LIVED HERE

Dublin's Great Georgian Squares

Dublin must boast some of the most splendidly photogenic doors in the world. Resplendent in high gloss technicolour with highly polished brass accoutrements, they are framed within marble lintels or ornamental pillars. They are there in abundance in Fitzwilliam Square, Merrion Square, and St. Stephen's Green in rows of once fashionable town houses of the Georgian Period. Now they are mainly the offices of doctors, solicitors and other professional men (or women) along with obscure societies of every persuasion.

Merrion Square is probably the most impressive. On one side is Leinster House (the present Parliament), the National Gallery, and the Natural History Museum, all set back from the road with manicured gardens and high wrought iron fences and gates. Down Mount Street, on one corner of Merrion Square, you can see the "Pepper Canister Church" more properly called St. Stephen's – another little gem. The quite splendid, enclosed Merrion Square park is much used by local office workers at lunchtime and open air concerts add to its outstanding botanical appeal. Flowers never seem to die here or leaves drift to where they shouldn't be and blades of grass seldom grow above the regulated length.

One of Dublins Fine Georgian Squares

FISH

Cockle and Mussel Medley with Garlic Dressing

110 grams/4 oz mussels.	110 grams/4 oz cooked
110 grams /4 oz cockles.	crabmeat.
225 grams/8 oz cooked	12 olives, (mixed black
prawn tails.	and green) with stones
225 grams/8 oz cooked	removed.
monktail, diced.	Fennel for garnish.

Dressing

150 ml/5 fl oz/⁵⁄₈ cup oil.	1 tblspn freshly chopped
75 ml/2½ fl oz/1/3 cup	chives.
wine vinegar.	Sugar, freshly ground
2 cloves garlic, crushed.	pepper and salt to
1 tblspn freshly chopped	taste.
parsley.	

Steam the mussels and cockles, (or cook in boiling water) to open the shells.
Combine all the fish and the olives in a bowl.
Mix together the ingredients for dressing and pour onto the fish. Leave to refrigerate for at least two hours before serving.
Serve as an entrée on a lettuce leaf and garnish with a tomato quarter and a piece of fennel.
SERVES 6

Crab with Mango and Avocado served with Lemon Dressing

2 avocadoes.	Lettuce.
1 mango.	4 spring onions,
120 ml/4 fl oz/½ cup	(chopped).
Lemon Dressing,	Freshly ground pepper
(recipe below).	to taste.
225 grams/8 oz crabmeat.	Chopped chives.

Peel and slice mango and avocado. Pour ½ the lemon dressing over. Arrange the crab on a bed of lettuce with mango and avocado slices. Refrigerate before serving. Sprinkle with chives and spring onions. Season to taste. Serve remaining dressing separately.

Lemon Dressing

120 ml/4 fl oz/½ cup	1 tspn paprika.
lemon juice.	1½ dessertspns sugar.
120 ml/4 fl oz/½ cup oil.	1 tspn salt.

Combine all the above ingredients. Shake well before using. Yield. 250 ml/8 fl oz/1 cup.
SERVES 4.

Dublin Bay Grilled Prawns

1 kg/2 lbs 3 oz Dublin Bay Prawns.
60 ml/2 fl oz/¼ cup oil.
2 lean rashers of bacon, cut into pieces.
2 onions, diced.
2 cups peeled tomatoes, halved.
120 ml/4 fl oz/½ cup fish stock.
1 tblspn white wine.
2 tblspns chopped parsley.
Chives. (optional).
Salt and freshly ground pepper to taste.
110 grams/4 oz Camembert cheese, cut into cubes.

Shell the prawns and set aside. Heat the oil and add bacon and diced onions. Add the tomatoes, stock, wine, parsley and chives. Simmer for ½ hour. Place in an ovenproof serving dish and put the Camembert and prawns on top. Place under grill until the cheese is melted.
Serve immediately.

Fillets of Sole St. Brigid

A tasty recipe with the compliments of Jameson's.

110 grams/4 oz mushrooms.
55 grams/2 oz onions.
110 grams/4 oz/½ cup butter.
4 fillets of sole.
120 ml/4 fl oz/½ cup Jameson's Irish Whiskey.
Fish Stock.
Chopped parsley.
2 tblspns flour.
1 egg, separated.
120 ml/4 fl oz/½ cup cream.
Salt.
Pepper.

Finely chop the mushrooms and onions and cook in half the butter. Lay the fillets with the top side down, pat them out with heavy knife or meat tenderiser. Spread the fillets with the mushroom and onion mixture. Fold the fillets over, place them in a buttered dish, add the Jameson's Irish Whiskey, a little chopped parsley and enough fish stock to cover. Season to taste with salt and pepper and poach until cooked.
Remove fish keep warm. Reduce the liquid to 600 ml/1 pint and thicken with the remaining butter and flour mixed together.
Cook for about 10 minutes, stirring all the time. Remove from heat, stir in the egg yolk and the cream. Cover the fillets of sole with the sauce and glaze under the grill.

Smoked Salmon Roulade

Base

55 grams/2 oz/¼ cup
  butter.
55 grams/2 oz/½ cup
  plain flour.
500 ml/16 fl oz/2 cups
  milk.
Salt and freshly ground
  pepper to taste.

1 tspn granulated sugar.
4 eggs, separated.

55 grams/2 oz smoked
  salmon cut into slices.
Fennel.

Melt butter, add flour and cook for 1-2 minutes. Gradually add the milk. Season if required. Add sugar and beaten egg yolks. Beat egg whites until stiff and fold into mixture. Line a baking tin 25 x 37.5 cm (10" x 15") with waxed paper. Grease and dust with flour, pour in the mixture bake at 170°C/325°F/Regulo 3 for about 40 minutes or until well risen, turn out immediately onto a clean teatowel, spread on the filling. Roll up as with a swiss roll. Place on a serving platter. Garnish with smoked salmon and fennel. Serve cold with sour cream.

Filling

225 grams/8 oz cream
  cheese.
350 ml/12 fl oz/1½ cups
  sour cream.

85 grams/3 oz smoked
  salmon.

Combine the cream cheese with just enough sour cream to make the mixture soft and spreadable. Fold in 55 grams/2 oz of the salmon. Refrigerate until needed.

Whole Salmon in Red Wine

1.8-2.3 kgs/4-5 lb salmon.
225 grams/8 oz button
  mushrooms.
2 bay leaves.
2 cloves.
Salt and pepper.
300ml/10 fl oz/1¼ cups
  red wine.

45 grams/1½ oz/3 tblspns
  butter.
45 grams/1½ oz/¼ cup
  flour.
150 ml/5 fl oz/⅔ cup
  cream (or half cream
  and half milk).

Wash and clean the fish. Remove the fins and head (head can be left on, if preferred) and place on foil on a shallow oven proof dish. Add the mushrooms, herbs and seasoning. Pour on the wine. Wrap loosely in foil and cook for about twenty minutes or until tender in 180°C/350°F/Regulo 4 oven. Do **not** over cook. Strain off the juices (keeping the mushrooms). Keep the fish warm. Make a roux with the flour, butter and some of the cooking juices. Add remaining juices, (and a little water if sauce is too thick). Stir in mushrooms and cream. Pour sauce over the salmon.
Decorate and serve hot.

Seafood Strudel with Pepper and Chives Sauce

10 sheets of filo pastry.
Melted butter.

2 large trout, boned and filleted.

Place the sheets of filo pastry on foil on a large baking tray, one leaf at a time brushing each leaf with butter. Place the trout fillets on the pastry. Pour over the Pepper and Chive Sauce, fold. Seal, and brush with melted butter. Bake at 200°C/400°F/Regulo 6 for 40-50 minutes.

Pepper and Chive Sauce.

30 grams/1 oz/2 tblspns butter.
30 grams/1 oz/2 tblspns flour.
600 ml/1 pint/2½ cups milk.
1 green pepper, finely chopped.

1 red pepper, finely chopped.
1 tblspn chives, chopped, (optional).
Salt and freshly ground pepper.

In a saucepan melt the butter. Stir in the flour and let cook over a low heat for 2-3 minutes. Add the milk and bring to the boil, stirring until sauce consistency. Add the chopped peppers, chives and season to taste.

Whole Plaice with Grapes

6 small whole plaice.
450 grams/1 lb green grapes.
300 ml/10 fl oz/1¼ cups white wine.
55 grams/2 oz/4 tblspns butter.
60 ml/2 fl oz/¼ cup lemon juice mixed with ½ cup cold water.

6 spring onions chopped.
2 tblspns flour.
120 ml/4 fl oz/½ cup warm milk.
120 ml/4 fl oz/½ cup cream.
2 bay leaves.
Seasoning.

Peel grapes and soak in white wine. Clean and wash the fish and place on a buttered baking dish. Pour the lemon juice and water over and the white wine drained from the grapes. Scatter the spring onions and bay leaves over and season. Dot on half the butter. Cover with foil and cook in 180°C/350°F/Regulo 4 oven for twenty minutes or until fish is just done. Carefully strain off the juices.
To prepare the sauce make roux of the flour and remaining butter. Add the strained fish juices slowly. Continue to cook and stir for five minutes over a low heat. Stir in the warm milk, bring to the boil, season and stir vigorously. Remove from the heat and gradually add the cream. Add the grapes and pour over the fish.
SERVES 6.

Fillo Envelopes

110 grams/4 oz/½ cup melted butter or margarine.
110 grams/4 oz Brie cheese.
6 dried apricots.
60 ml/2 fl oz/¼ cup orange juice.
1 large avocado.
6 sheets Fillo pastry.
Seasoning.

Boil the apricots in the orange juice for 3-5 minutes, let cool. Place one sheet of fillo on a flat surface, brush lightly with melted butter. Fold in half lengthwise. Lightly butter again. Divide the cheese and avocado into six pieces and place one piece of each with an apricot on the end of the pastry. Season. Take a corner of the pastry and fold into a triangle enclosing the three ingredients. Fold into a second triangle and repeat until this whole sheet of pastry is used and the filling is well enclosed.

Repeat this procedure 5 more times. Brush with melted butter and bake at 180°C/350°F/ Regulo 4 for 15-20 minutes.

Serve hot with fish.

Sea Trout Strudel with Hot Tartare Sauce

2-3 Sea Trout fillets, medium size.
300 ml/½ pint/1¼ cups Tartare Sauce.
10 large sheets Fillo Pastry.
110 grams/4 oz/½ cup butter, (melted).

Spread the first sheet of fillo onto a table. Brush with some melted butter and cover with the next sheet. Repeat this until all the fillo is used up. Put trout fillets on top. Cover with sauce. Brush all edges with butter and fold into the shape of a strudel. Sealing ends well, brush liberally with melted butter. Prick some air holes in the top and bake in a hot oven for 45 minutes or until well brown.

Fish may be tested by poking a skewer into one of the holes.

Hot Tartare Sauce

600 ml/1 pint/2½ cups milk.
1 medium onion, sliced.
3 black peppercorns.
55 grams/2 oz/¼ cup butter.
55 grams/2 oz/scant ½ cup flour.
2 tspns finely chopped capers.
4 tspns finely chopped gherkins.
½ tspn tumeric.
Pinch mace.
Salt and freshly ground pepper.

Heat the milk with the onion, and peppercorns. Slowly, bring to the boil stirring all the time. Remove from heat and strain and leave for 30 minutes. In a separate saucepan melt the butter, add the flour and cook for 2-3 minutes but do not allow to brown. Gradually add the strained milk stirring all the time, until the sauce is of a thick consistency. Lastly, add the capers, gherkins, mace, tumeric and seasoning. Serve remaining sauce separately.

Parfait of Seafood with Avocado Sauce

This dish is one of the indulgences available at the Shelbourne and the recipe was given to me by the chef.

Mousse

225 grams/8 oz brill.
1 egg white.
100 ml/3½ fl oz/⅜ cup brandy.
50 ml/2 fl oz/scant ¼ cup vermouth.
300 ml/10 fl oz/1¼ cups cream.

110 grams/4 oz fillet of sole.
55 grams/2 oz scallop roe.
6 spinach leaves.
85 grams/3 oz salmon.
85 grams/3 oz scallops.
Seasoning.
10 Prawns or mussels.

To make the mousse:

Pass the cooked brill through a fine sieve. Place in a bowl on ice and fold in the egg white, brandy and vermouth. Season then fold in the cream. Let it set for ½ hour.

Season the sole and line a terrine dish with half the fillets. Put a quarter of the mousse into the terrine and season. Place the scallop roe on a spinach leaf and set on top of the mousse in the dish. Then slice the salmon into strips and place on the scallop roe. Cover with spinach leaves and place half the remaining mousse on top.
Complete by adding the rest of the spinach leaves followed by the scallops, the rest of the mousse onto this, and finally the prawns.
Lastly, cover with remainder of sole fillets. Sounds complicated, but it's really very easy!
Place the terrine in a pot of boiling water (without submerging fully) and cook for 30 minutes.
Remove from the water and place a weight on top to extract excess juices. Cook for a further ¾ hour in a bain-marie in the oven, removing excess juices as necessary.
Finally, allow to cool for 3 hours.
Slice very finely to serve.

Avocado Sauce

3 avocadoes.
30 grams/1 oz shallots/ spring onions.
Juice of ½ lemon.
½ bay leaf.
Seasoning.
100 ml/3½ fl oz/⅜ cup vermouth.

Pinch of nutmeg.
250 ml/8 fl oz/1 cup fish stock.
30 grams/1 oz/2 tblspns butter.

Peel and dice the avocadoes, dice the shallots, place these in a pan, add the lemon juice, bay leaf, salt and pepper, vermouth and nutmeg. Cook for 3 minutes, then add to fish stock and cook for 4 minutes. Fold in the butter and blend thoroughly.
Present on a plate with the sauce around the Seafood Parfait.

Gandon's Dublin

The architect James Gandon, in the last two decades of the 18th century conceived three buildings (part of one and the whole of two!) of enormous presence.

Two of them can be seen easily from O'Connell Bridge which spans the River Liffey. Look downstream and you'll not miss the Custom's House with its green copper dome standing proudly on the north bank of the river. Now face upstream, and keeping an eye out for that hallmark of Gandon – a green dome – you will see the Four Courts, one of the most handsome Court Houses in the business.

Leaving the bridge behind you and walking south you enter Westmoreland Street: walk a further 100 yards and on your right is the Bank of Ireland – an ex-Parliament House for which Gandon designed the portico that faces onto the street.

One of the conditions of the sale to the Bank of Ireland (1803) was that they obliterate all memory of the building's parliamentary past. The bankers, knowing a good thing when they saw one, disregarded the stipulation and the porter will show you, if you are interested, the Chamber where the House of Lords sat in cloistered splendour.

Apart from the pubs, Gandon's two great buildings on the Liffey banks seem to be amongst the few major buildings in Dublin to function for the purpose for which they were built.

House of Lords in The Bank of Ireland.

MAIN COURSES

Chicken with Mangoes

1 Chicken. 1.350-1.8 kg/ 3-4 lb, jointed.
30 grams/1 oz/2 tblspns butter.
6 slices mango, sliced (or tinned may be used).
3 small onions.
1 lemon grated.
300 ml/10 fl oz/1¼ cups chicken stock.
Juice of ½ lemon.
Salt and freshly ground pepper.
120 ml/4 fl oz/½ cup cream.
Pinch of grated nutmeg.

Fry the chicken pieces in half the butter until sealed all over. Set aside. Melt remaining butter in casserole and sweat onions over medium heat. Add mango and cook for a further 3 minutes. Add chicken pieces, lemon rind and stock. Cover and cook at 180°C/ 350°F/Regulo 4 for 1 hour or until chicken pieces are tender.
Remove chicken pieces, keep warm. Skim off any excess fat from the juices. Add lemon juice and season to taste. Stir in the cream and bring to a gentle simmer. Lastly add a pinch of nutmeg and pour over the chicken. Serve immediately.
SERVES 4-6

Cold Chicken with Yoghurt, Herbs and Kiwifruit Mayonnaise

1.4 kgs/3 lb chicken.
30 grams/1 oz/2 tblspns butter.
4 sprigs fresh coriander or ¼ tspn dried.
½ orange, quartered and peeled.
4 kiwifruit.
60 ml/2 fl oz/4 tblspns natural yoghurt.
150 ml/¼ pint/⅔ cup thick mayonnaise.
Lettuce.
Salt & pepper.

Cream the butter with some seasoning and coriander. Smear the chicken with some of the butter. Put the rest of the butter with the orange pieces, inside the chicken. Roast at 190°C/375°F/Regulo 5 for about 1 hour 20 minutes. Drain chicken and set aside to cool. Skim off any fat (reserving the juices). Let cool.
To serve: peel and dice two kiwifruit. Combine with the yoghurt, mayonnaise, and chicken juices. Add seasoning to taste. Cut cold chicken into pieces and arrange on a serving plate with crisp lettuce. Spoon over some of the dressing and pour the remainder into a dish to serve separately. Decorate with remaining kiwifruit, (sliced).
SERVES 4-6.

Lamb Cutlets with Pineapple, Barbecue Style

2 tblspns soft brown
  sugar.
30 ml/2 tblspns soy sauce.
30 ml/2 tblspns white
  wine vinegar.
Pinch of five spice
  powder.
2 tblspns vegetable oil.
Salt and freshly ground
  pepper.

4 lamb cutlets.
55 grams/2 oz
  mushrooms.
2 rashers bacon, diced.
110 grams/4 oz/½ cup
  pineapple.
Watercress and croûtons
  to garnish.

In a shallow dish mix together the brown sugar, soy sauce, white wine vinegar, five spice powder, vegetable oil and seasoning.
Place the cutlets in dish and turn to coat in the marinade. Leave for 2 hours.
Cook the mushrooms and bacon lightly, add the pineapple for the last minute. Drain the cutlets and place under a high grill and cook for five minutes either side. Top with chopped mushrooms, bacon and pineapple. Spoon over the remaining marinade and grill for a further 1½ minutes. Garnish with watercress and croûtons.
SERVES 4.

Rack of Wicklow Lamb with Honey and Herbs

2 rib racks of lamb,
  (of 6 cutlets each).
Knob of butter.

2 dessertspns honey.
Mixed herbs.

Place rack of lamb on a baking tray. Wrap foil around the tops of the bones to prevent burning. Rub with the butter and drizzle with honey. Lastly sprinkle on mixed herbs. Bake at 180°C/350°F/Regulo 4. for about 45 minutes, basting frequently. Skim the fat off and serve remaining juices separately.
Serve with Mint Jelly.
SERVES 6.

IN
No 7 HOEY'S COVRT
(now demolished)
about 100 feet NW of this spot
it is reputed that
**JONATHAN
SWIFT**
DEAN OF ST. PATRICK'S
CATHEDRAL.
WAS BORN
on the 30th day of Nov.
1667
HE DIED ON THE 19TH
DAY OF OCT 1745.
MCMXII

Pork Fillets and Avocado with Cheese Sauce

1 kg/2lb 3oz pork (approx 2 pork fillets).

3 ripe avocadoes, (peeled and sliced).

Split the pork fillets down centre and flatten slightly. Roast for 30 minutes at 180°C/350°F/Regulo 4. Remove from the oven and cover with avocadoes. Immediately spoon over the cheese sauce and sprinkle remaining cheese on top. Put under grill until the cheese has melted. The avocadoes should be just warm, but not cooked.
Serve immediately.

Cheese Sauce

55 grams/2 oz/¼ cup butter.

55 grams/2 oz/½ cup plain flour.

600 ml/1 pint/2½ cups milk.

225 grams/8 oz grated cheese.

Salt and freshly ground pepper.

A little made mustard

In a saucepan, melt the butter and stir in the flour. Cook for 2-3 minutes to cook the flour. Over a moderate heat, add the milk, stirring all the time until of a thick consistency. Stir in mustard and 140 grams/5 oz of the grated cheese. Season if desired.

Loin of Pork, with Honey Glaze

1.8 kgs/4 lb loin of pork with bones removed.
Salt, as needed.
Five spice powder.
2 tblspns oil.
1 tblspn honey.
2 dessertspns soy sauce.
85 ml/3 fl oz/⅓ cup orange juice.

1 rind of 1 orange, grated.
1 tspn freshly grated ginger.
1 tspn cornflour.
2 tblspns water.

Score rind of pork well. Mix together 1 dessertspn salt and a good pinch of five spice powder and rub this over the inside of pork. Roll up and tie with the rind uppermost. Rub extra salt and oil over the rind. Cook at 220°C/425°F/Regulo 7 for 15 minutes or until the pork starts to crackle. Reduce to 180°C/350°F/Regulo 4 and cook for a further hour. Combine honey, soy sauce, orange juice and rind, and ginger. Pour this over the pork. Bake a further 15-20 minutes, basting frequently until cooked through.
Remove meat from dish and keep warm. Pour juices into a saucepan. Allow to settle and skim off any fat. Combine cornflour and water and add to the juices. Stir over a medium heat until the sauce thickens.

From left to right: Loin of Pork, with Honey Glaze, Dublin Bay Grilled Prawns, Cold Chicken with Yoghurt etc., Cockle & Mussel Medley with Garlic Dressing, Chicken with Mangoes.

Royal Hospital, Kilmainham

History tells us that a gentleman called William Robinson designed the very splendid Royal Hospital at Kilmainham. It was built between 1680 and 1685, the brainchild of the then Duke of Ormond, as a home for pensioner soldiers.

The old soldiers have long gone elsewhere and the building has since been used variously as an overflow store for the National Gallery, a Garda barracks and a resting place for derelict outmoded statues of British vintage. One statue of Queen Victoria has also departed elsewhere – to a place of honour in Sydney, Australia

This great stone hospital has now been recycled into a multipurpose, cultural and exhibition centre and a venue where visiting dignitaries can be entertained in considerable splendour.

The Chapel in the Royal Hospital, Kilmainham.

VEGETABLES

Baked Onions with Walnuts

3 large onions.
30 grams/1 oz/2 tblspns
  butter.
250 ml/8 fl oz/1 cup stock.
1 tspn lemon rind.
1 dessertspn honey.
Seasoning.
Paprika.
55 grams/2 oz/½ cup
  walnuts.

Peel the onions and cut in half. Arrange in a baking dish. Over a low heat, combine butter, stock, lemon rind, honey, and a dash of paprika. Season as required. Pour over the onions, cover with foil and bake at 180°C/350°F/Regulo 4. for 45 minutes to 1 hour or until tender. Sprinkle the walnuts over and bake a further 10 minutes to crisp the nuts.

SERVES 6

Colcannon

The word "colcannon" comes from the Irish word cāl ceannan literally meaning: white headed cabbage.

750 grams/1 lb 11 oz
  cabbage.
500 grams/1 lb 2 oz
  potatoes.
Small bunch spring
  onions.
170 ml/6 fl oz/¾ cup milk.
⅛ tspn nutmeg.
Salt, freshly ground
  black pepper.
55-85 grams/2-3 oz/
  4-6 tblspns butter.

Cut the cabbage into quarters and cook in salted, boiling water until just tender. Drain and cool. Boil the potatoes until tender; drain and mash.
Dice the spring onions. Simmer the white part in the milk until tender. Add both milk and spring onions to the mashed potato, beat until smooth. Dice the cabbage and add to the potato. Season. Pile into serving dish, make a well in the centre and add the butter. Serve immediately, very hot.

JOSEPH SHERIDAN
LE FANU

1814 – 1873

WRITER
LIVED HERE

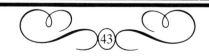

Hot Potato Salad

1 kg/2 lb 3 oz/
new potatoes.
4 tblspns chopped
parsley.
4 tblspns chopped
spring onions.
1 tblspn chopped chives.
2 tblspns tinned or
bottled green
peppercorns.

2 tblspns mayonnaise.
2 tblspns French
dressing.
120 ml/4 fl oz/½ cup
cream.
¼ tspn salt

Steam the potatoes until cooked. Combine the remaining ingredients in a pan and heat. Add the potatoes and cook for a further five minutes.

Garlic Parsnips in Sour Cream

1 kg/2 lbs 3 oz parsnips.
½ tspn salt.
¼ tspn pepper.
2 cloves garlic.

15 grams/½ oz/1 tblspn
butter.
250ml/8 fl oz/1 cup
sour cream.

Peel the parsnips and cut into cubes. Cook until soft and mash. Add salt and pepper. Fry the garlic in the butter being careful not to let it burn. Add sour cream. Pour onto mashed parsnips and beat well. Heat the mixture through before serving. Goes well with cold meat.

Trinity College

Across the road from the Bank of Ireland on College Green (originally called Hoggen Green) stands Trinity College, the University of Dublin. It was founded by Elizabeth I in 1592 for, amongst other things, the 'planting of learning'.

Since then various buildings have been added to the college, many being outstanding examples of their period. A particularly worthy example is the 300 ft Palladian façade (1752-59): it is one of Dublin's finest. All of the original buildings have unfortunately long since disappeared.

The oldest still standing is the Rubrics – dating back to the time of Queen Anne (1700) – now used as residences.

The organ, in the theatre (or Examination Hall), has an intriguing history. Built in the Netherlands, it was captured from a Spanish ship in 1702 and acquired by the Duke of Ormond, who was then serving in the British fleet. He later presented it to the College.

The old Library was completed in 1732. On the first floor is the Long Room. Sombre, barrel vaulted and still one of the most impressive interiors in Dublin. It is quite massive with an immense display of books and reputedly the largest reading room in Europe. The Library is now the home of a number of treasures, the principle one being the "Book of Kells", a magnificently illustrated copy of the Gospels, dating from the 9th century. The artist was an unknown monk. Other documents include the Book of Durrow (7th century and the earliest of the collection), the Book Dimma (8th century) and the Book of Armagh.

One of Trinity's most famous sons was George Berkeley; philosopher, economist, mathematician, physicist and Bishop. Bishop Berkeley was born in 1685, entered the College in 1700, graduated in 1704 and was elected a Fellow of the College in 1707 at the age of 22. He was presented at court in London by Jonathan Swift.

He is well known in the field of philosophy for having advanced a new theory of sense perception and for his so-called denial of the existence of matter.

He was largely misunderstood in his time, it being thought that he held that material objects existed through being perceived, and that if no one was perceiving them they didn't exist. To the criticism that objects would always have to be leaping in and out of existence in order to be observed, his reply was that God is constantly perceiving everything and that this holds all things in existence.

In view of the new theories in physics, which view the ultimate atomic particles as energy rather than matter, he may have been prophetic!

Anyway, a limerick by Ronald Knox was supposed to set forth Berkeley's theory of material objects!

There was a young man who said "God,
Must think it exceedingly odd,
   If he finds that this tree,
   Continues to be,
When there's no one about in the Quad".

Reply

Dear Sir:
   Your astonishment's odd:
   I am always about in the Quad
   And that's why the tree
   Will continue to be,
   Since observed by
      Yours faithfully
        God.

The Long Room, Trinity College Library.

DESSERTS

Lemon Cups

30 grams/1 oz/
¼ cup flour.
225 grams/8 oz/1 cup
castor sugar.
2 tblspns vegetable oil.
Pinch of salt.
2 tspns grated lemon
peel.

85 ml/2½ fl oz/⅓ cup
lemon juice.
350 ml/12 fl oz/1½ cups
milk, scalded.
3 egg yolks, (beaten).
3 egg whites, (whisked).

Beat together the flour, sugar, oil and salt. Add lemon peel and juice. Stir milk into the egg yolk and add to the lemon mixture. Lastly fold in egg whites. Pour into 150 ml/5 fl oz/¼ cup ramekins. Put ramekins into a bain-marie 2.5 cm (1 inch) deep and bake at 170°C/325°F/ Regulo 3-4. for 30-40 minutes or until a skewer comes out clean. Serve immediately.

SERVES 6.

Guinness Christmas Pudding

285 grams/10 oz/6 cups
fresh breadcrumbs.
225 grams/8 oz/1 cup soft
brown sugar.
225 grams/8 oz/1¾ cups
currants.
285 grams/10 oz/2½ cups
shredded suet.
½ tspn salt.

1 tspn mixed spice.
1 lemon, grated.
1 dessertspn lemon juice.
2 large eggs (beaten).
150 ml/¼ pint/⅔ cup
milk.
300 ml/½ pint/1¼ cups
Guinness.

Mix together in a large basin all the dry ingredients. Stir in the lemon rind and juice, eggs, milk and Guinness. Mix well and turn into two 1.5 litre/2½ pint/6 cup pudding basins.
Tie pudding cloths over puddings or cover them tightly with grease-proof and foil. Leave overnight. Steam for about seven and a half hours.
If you're not eating it immediately, cool, recover and store in a cool place.
When required, steam for 2-3 hours before serving.

Gateau Emo

This light ice cream cake is an easy dessert to make and can be made ahead of time but needs to be thawed a little before serving.

1 tin evaporated milk.
110 grams/4 oz/½ cup sugar.
1 round sponge cake.
Juice and zest of 1 lemon.
Fruit and fresh cream to decorate.

Put the tin of milk in the freezer for 3-4 hours until very cold or refrigerate overnight.
Beat the very cold milk with the sugar until double in bulk. Add the lemon zest and juice, a little at a time until the milk thickens.
Slice the sponge horizontally into 3-4 sections. Put one section into an 18.5 cm (7 inches) spring-form tin.
Put on a thick layer of milk mixture. Repeat layers of sponge and milk mixture until sponge is used up – ending with a thin layer of milk mixture for the top. Cover with cling-film. Freeze.
About an hour before serving, remove from tin. Pipe on some fresh cream and decorate with fresh fruit or fruit glaze.
Leave cake in the fridge, *not* freezer before serving to let it soften a little.

Downunder Christmas Pudding

In Australia many people find the traditional Christmas Pudding too solid in mid Summer and have invented a frozen Christmas Pudding which is more suitable to the hot climate. You might like to try this Downunder version for a change.

70 grams/2½ oz/½ cup sultanas.
70 grams/2½ oz/½ cup raisins.
45 grams/1½ oz/¼ cup glacé cherries, whole.
45 grams/1½ oz/¼ cup other glacé fruit.
55 grams/2 oz/⅓ cup mixed peel.
120 ml/4 fl oz/½ cup whiskey.
30 grams/1 oz/¼ cup almonds, halved.
30 grams/1 oz/½ cup coconut.
1 litre/1¾ pints vanilla ice-cream.
120 ml/4 fl oz/½ cup cream.
Extra cream to serve, (optional).

Combine the dried and glacé fruits with the whiskey and leave to soak overnight.
Soften the icecream a little and mix in the fruits, almonds, coconut and cream. Transfer to a pudding basin. Cover tightly and freeze until firm.
Dip into boiling water for a second to unmould onto a serving plate. Pour thickened cream over and top with a sprig of holly.

Cream Cheese Slice

450 grams/1 lb puff
  pastry.
450 grams/1 lb/2 cups
  unsalted butter.
450 grams/1 lb/2 cups
  castor sugar.
340 grams/12 oz/1½ cups
  cream cheese.
170 ml/6 fl oz/¾ cup
  hot water.

2 tspns gelatine.
2 tblspns lemon butter,
  (lemon curd).
½ tspn vanilla essence.
55 grams/2 oz/scant
  ½ cup icing   sugar.
Few drops yellow
  colouring, (optional).

Roll pastry to 4 mm (1/6 inch) thick and cut into two 30 cm /(12 inch) squares. Place onto an ungreased scone tray and prick thoroughly with a fork. Bake at 200°C/400°F/Regulo 6 for 15-20 minutes or until pale brown in colour. Let cool. Put the two pieces of pastry together to trim the edges to the same size. Cream the butter, sugar and cream cheese. Add 4 tblspns of the hot water and continue to beat until light and fluffy. Dissolve gelatine in remaining hot water. Add gradually and beat in thoroughly. If the mixture becomes too soft, place in refrigerator for a few minutes to firm. Divide mixture in half. To one half add the lemon butter (curd) with a few drops of yellow colouring. Mix a few drops of vanilla essence into the remainder.Spread the lemon cheese filling onto one sheet of pastry and cover with the vanilla filling. Place the second piece of pastry on top and press down firmly. Place in the refrigerator for 3-4 hours. Dust the top of the slice liberally with sifted icing sugar and cut into squares.

Raisin Pie

450 grams/1 lb
  sweet pie pastry.
Grated rind and juice of
  one large lemon.
Grated rind and juice of
  one large orange.
110 grams/4 oz/½ cup
  sugar.

300 grams/10 oz/2 cups
  seedless raisins.
400 ml/14 fl oz/1¾ cups
  water.
4 tblspns flour.
Egg for glazing.

Mix the flour with a little of the water to a smooth paste. Combine the lemon and orange juice and rind, sugar, raisins and remaining water in a saucepan, and bring to the boil. Reduce heat. Add the flour and water mixture and stir. Cook gently for about five minutes, stirring constantly.
Line a deep 23 cm/9 inch pie tin with pastry, pour in the filling and top with pastry. Paint with beaten egg, and bake for 45 minutes at 200°C/400°F Regulo 6 oven. Lower the heat a little if the pie is getting too brown. Dust with icing sugar.
Serve hot or cold.

From the left: Emo Gateau, Downunder Christmas Pudding, Cream Cheese Slice.

History of Dublin

This splendidly sited city was in the news as far back as 140 A.D. In that year Ptolemy observed that the settlers of Eblana (now Dublin) were a force to be reckoned with. The settlement remained until the invading Vikings arrived some 700 years later. Settling on the banks of the Liffey they used their new found site as a centre for trade, and as a base from which to launch their forays into the interior. Dublin (or Dyfflin as the Norsemen called it), soon became recognised as a commercial asset and battles raged on and off up until 1171 for ownership of the Viking stronghold. In that year the Vikings assembled a fleet of 60 ships and warriors, to defend themselves from yet another attack, but they lost the day and their leader Hascalf was executed.

This marked the end of the Viking era but ironically, though this was the end of an occupation by one set of foreigners, they were to be replaced by another lot! Routing of the Norsemen gave Henry II of England the excuse to visit Ireland with a sizeable force, and thus from a position of strength was able to secure the loyalty of the Irish chiefs. The city was granted its first charter and became the acclaimed capital of Ireland.

Like most medieval cities, Dublin suffered the usual setbacks such as civil unrest, fire and horrendous epidemics. (In 1650, the plague alone killed some 16,000 citizens). Despite this, the city prospered and had amenities such as piped water, paved streets and lighting before many of its European counterparts.

The 17th century saw a consolidation of English power in Ireland, and the 18th and 19th centuries were ones of great prosperity.

However, the 20th century heralded an end to English rule. In 1922, Dublin became the capital of an independent 26 county Irish Free State. In 1937 the Free State became Eire and in 1948 The Republic of Ireland. In 1972 Ireland joined the European Economic Community.

Dublin's millenium in 1988 resulted in an upsurge of the city's appreciation of its heritage and a rejuvenation and beautification programme unparalleled in its history.

New buildings which were allowed to smother significant Viking remains or which replaced handsome Georgian mansions might justify their existence if they are around for the bimillenium in 2988. They have caused eyebrows to be raised which might be a long time coming down.

This convivial 1000-year-old city remains a happily ageless and much loved city by those who know it well.

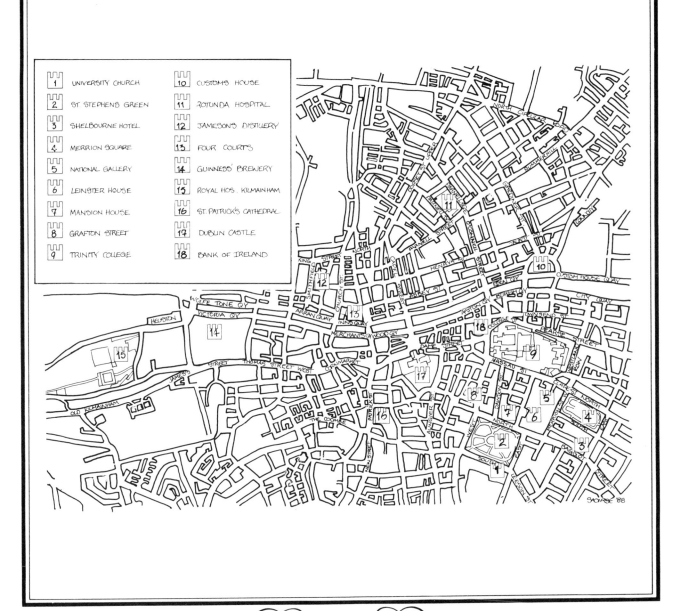

1	UNIVERSITY CHURCH	10	CUSTOMS HOUSE
2	ST STEPHENS GREEN	11	ROTUNDA HOSPITAL
3	SHELBOURNE HOTEL	12	JAMESON'S DISTILLERY
4	MERRION SQUARE	13	FOUR COURTS
5	NATIONAL GALLERY	14	GUINNESS' BREWERY
6	LEINSTER HOUSE	15	ROYAL HOS. KILMAINHAM
7	MANSION HOUSE	16	ST. PATRICK'S CATHEDRAL
8	GRAFTON STREET	17	DUBLIN CASTLE
9	TRINITY COLLEGE	18	BANK OF IRELAND

SAOIRSE '88

FRUIT SALADS

Fruit Salad with Toasted Almonds

1 large pineapple, cut into pieces. (2 medium cans of pineapple may be used if fresh is not available).

6 mandarins, segmented, (tinned may be used).

110 grams/4 oz grapes, black and green.

3 bananas, cut into pieces.

120 ml/4 fl oz/½ cup orange juice.

55 grams/2 oz/½ cup blanched almonds, to decorate.

250 ml/8 fl oz/1 cup ginger ale.

Soak the bananas in the orange juice. Arrange fruits in a serving dish so that each fruit is separate from the other. Pour ginger ale and orange juice over. Grill almonds until lightly browned and sprinkle on top.

Winter Fruit Salad

225 grams/8 oz/1¼ cups dried apricots.

170 grams/6 oz/1 cup prunes.

3 figs.

750 ml/25 fl oz/3 cups orange juice.

70 grams/2½ oz/½ cup sultanas.

2 tspns grated orange rind.

1-2 dessertspns rum.

1 tspn cinnamon.

¾ tspn grated nutmeg.

300 ml/10 fl oz/1¼ cups cream, whipped.

Brown sugar.

Soak the apricots, prunes and figs in the orange juice overnight.

Following day put the orange juice and fruits over a gentle heat with the sultanas, orange rind, rum, cinnamon and nutmeg. Simmer until soft. Cool, remove stones from prunes.

Place in an ovenproof serving dish. Spread fresh cream on top, sprinkle with brown sugar and place under a preheated grill *only until the sugar caramelises.*

Berry Salad

450 grams/1 lb raspberries.
450 grams/1 lb blackcurrants.
450 grams/1 lb black cherries, (tinned if necessary).

450 grams/1 lb loganberries.
250 ml/8 fl oz/1 cup red wine.
Orange zest.
Blanched almonds.

Prepare the fruit and mix together in serving dish. Add the red wine. Sweeten. Decorate with orange zest and blanched almonds.

Melon Salad with Brandy and Wine

½ small watermelon.
1 cantaloupe melon.
1 punnet strawberries.
2 fresh peaches.

3 tblspns brandy.
250 ml/8 fl oz/1 cup sweet dessert wine.

Prepare the fruit and put into a bowl. Sprinkle with icing sugar and pour brandy and wine over. Serve cold.

Citrus Salad

1 x 530 gram/1 lb 3 oz tin grapefruit segments, (unsweetened).
2 x 225 gram/8 oz

tins mandarins, (unsweetened or in light syrup).
6 dessertspns Curaçao.

Drain the fruits. Cut grapefruit into small pieces and mix with mandarins. Divide into six individual serving dishes and pour 1 dessertspn of Curaçao over each.

Grapefruit St. Patrick

This makes a perfect starter for a formal meal.

1.2 kgs/2 lb 10 oz tin unsweetened grapefruit segments, (or equivalent in fresh grapefruit with pith removed).

2 tblspns finely chopped mint.
Sifted icing sugar.

Cut the grapefruit into bite size pieces and mix in the mint. Divide into 6 glass serving dishes. Lightly sprinkle with icing sugar and garnish with a sprig of mint or shamrock.

Hot Banana and Orange Salad

For a more "spirited" dessert, sherry, brandy or rum may be added.

4 bananas.	1 tblspn brown sugar.
2 tspns orange rind.	30 grams/1 oz/2 tblspns
8 orange segments.	butter.
2 tblspns orange juice.	1 tspn cinnamon.

Peel and slice the bananas lengthwise. Pour on orange juice. Place on a buttered ovenproof dish. Sprinkle on coarsely grated orange rind and arrange orange segments on top. Dot with butter and sprinkle on brown sugar and cinnamon.
Cook in a hot oven 200°C/400°F/Regulo 6 for fifteen minutes. Finish off under the grill.
SERVES 4.

Tutti Frutti

This brandied fruit salad is a good standby to use as a topping or to serve with vanilla ice cream. I make it fresh every year.

In a large glass or stone jar (not airtight) put one cup of brandy and one cup of sugar. Add fruit as it comes in season and is at its best – cherries, strawberries, plums, apricots, peaches, apples, pears etc. Cut into small pieces. Add no more sugar or brandy. Be sure to stir after each addition.

St. Patrick's Cathedral Choir School. Founded 1432 A.D.

From top left: Fruit Salad with Toasted Almonds, Winter Fruit Salad, Berry Salad, Citrus Salad.

Leinster House

Leinster House (previously known as Kildare House) was designed by Richard Cassels for James Fitzgerald, Lord Kildare, who succeeded to the title at the age of 22.

As his former house in Suffolk Street did not satisfy him, he bought a piece of land in the then less fashionable part of Coote Lane (known today as Kildare Street).

In 1745 he commenced building a palace which was completed in 1748. This huge town-built country house was renamed Leinster House when the Earl of Kildare became the Duke of Leinster in 1766.

It is believed by some experts to be the prototype for the White House in Washington D.C. which was designed by the Irish architect, James Hoban in 1780.

It was not until the twentieth century, however, that it really came into its own. Today it is the seat of Dáil Éireann (House of Representatives) and Seanad Éireann (the Senate). These two bodies, along with the State President make up the Oireachtas (National Parliament).

The formal grounds are best viewed from Merrion Square. Despite additions of twentieth century technology and the ringing of division bells for its now more functional use the beauty and splendour of the building still survive.

Had he spar'd his tongue and pen, he might have rose like other men.
"Verses on the death of Dr Swift." Dean Jonathan Swift, 1667-1745.

Leinster House

CAKES

New Style Fruit Cake

110 grams/4 oz/¾ cup green glacé cherries, halved.
110 grams/4 oz/⅔ cup red glacé cherries, whole.
70 grams/2½ oz/½ cup sultanas.
100 grams/3½ oz/⅔ cup mixed peel.
225 grams/8 oz/2 cups chopped dates.
225 grams/8 oz/2 cups broken walnuts.

225 grams/8 oz/1½ cups whole Brazil nuts.
85 grams/3 oz/¾ cup plain flour.
½ tspn baking powder.
Pinch salt.
3 eggs, beaten.
1 tspn vanilla essence.
170 grams/6 oz/¾ cup castor sugar.

Grease and line a 18 cm (7 inch) cake tin. Combine the nuts and the fruit. Sift together the flour, baking powder and salt and mix through the fruit mixture. Add the vanilla and sugar to the eggs and fold through the fruit. Spoon mixture into prepared tin and bake at 150°C/300°F/Regulo 2 for 1-1½ hours. Press down.

The top may be decorated with extra whole fruit and nuts and a sugar glaze to make it look more festive. For sugar glaze boil together 1 cup of sugar to 1 cup of water until it becomes a syrup.

Guinness Cake

225 grams/8 oz/1 cup butter.
225 grams/8 oz/1 cup brown sugar.
4 eggs, lightly beaten.
285 grams/10 oz/2 cups plain flour and 2 tspns of mixed spice sieved together.

225 grams/8 oz/1½ cups seedless raisins.
225 grams/8 oz/1½ cups sultanas.
110 grams/4 oz/½ cup mixed peel.
8-12 tblspns Guinness.
110 grams/4 oz/1 cup walnuts.

Cream the butter and sugar together until light and creamy.

Gradually beat in the eggs. Fold in the flour and mixed spice. Then add the raisins, sultanas, mixed peel and walnuts. Mix well. Stir 4 tblspns of Guinness into the mixture. Mix to a soft dropping consistency. Turn into a prepared 18 cm (7 inch) cake tin. Bake in a very moderate oven: 180°C/350°F/Regulo 4. for 1 hour. Then reduce heat to a cool oven: 160°C/325°F/Regulo 3 and cook for another 1½ hours.

Allow it to become cold. Remove from cake tin. Prick the base of the cake with a skewer and spoon over the remaining 4-8 tblspns of Guinness.

Keep the cake for at least 1 week before serving.

Banana Cake

3 small ripe bananas.
1 tspn baking soda.
55 grams/2 oz/¼ cup
   butter.
225 grams/8 oz/
   1 cup sugar.
1 egg, beaten.

1 tspn baking powder.
170 grams/6 oz/1½ cups
   flour (plain).
1 tspn cinnamon.
1 tspn mixed spice.
2 tblspns milk.

Mash the bananas. Add the baking soda and set aside for one hour.
Cream the butter and sugar, add the well beaten egg and banana. Mix well. Add sifted baking powder, flour, cinnamon, and mixed spice. Mix well, and finally add 2 tblspns of milk. Put into greased loaf tin.
Place in a moderate oven - 180°C/350°F/ Regulo 4 for 30-45 minutes. Cool on a wire rack.

Icing

10 tblspns icing sugar,
   (sifted).
Lemon juice as needed.

55 grams/2 oz/
   ¼ cup butter.

Cream the butter and icing sugar. Add lemon juice, until of desired consistency. Spread onto Banana Cake and sprinkle with cinnamon.

Carrot Cake

When Carrot Cake was served where I worked in Australia, it soon became a popular treat with morning coffee or afternoon tea. Time and time again new customers arrived to sample the Carrot Cake!

250 ml/8 fl oz/1 cup oil.
140 grams/5 oz/ ⅔ cup
   raw sugar
2 eggs, beaten.
225 grams/8 oz/1½ cups
   wholemeal self raising
   flour.

3 tspns cinnamon.
¾ tspn baking soda.
3 cups grated carrot.
55 grams/2 oz/ ½ cup
   walnuts.

Beat the oil and sugar and add the eggs. Stir in the flour, cinnamon, baking soda. Lastly stir in the grated carrot and walnuts. Pour into a greased 20 cm (8 inch) square tin. Bake at 180°C/350°F/Regulo 4 for 50-60 minutes or until soft and spongy. Remove and leave to cool on a wire tray.

Icing

110 grams/4 oz/½ cup
   cream cheese.
55 grams/2 oz/ ¼ cup
   butter or margarine.

110-170 grams/4-6 oz/
   ¾-1¼ cups sifted icing
   sugar.

Beat together cream cheese and butter. Add icing sugar and beat again until all is incorporated. Spread onto cooled cake.

Angel's Hair Cake

It doesn't look like carrots. It looks quite spectacular and tastes heavenly.

Angel's Hair

225 grams/8 oz grated
    carrot.   **Juice of 1 lemon.**
225 grams/8 oz/1 cup sugar.

Put the grated carrot in a pan and cover with water. Bring to the boil and let simmer until just tender. Stir in the sugar and half the lemon juice. Cook for a further 5-10 minutes or until the carrots are candied. Add remaining lemon juice.

For the cake

110 grams/4 oz/   Pinch salt.
  ½ cup butter.   1 tblspn milk.
2 eggs.   ½ tspn vanilla essence.
110 grams/4 oz/ ½ cup
  castor sugar.   Whipped cream.
170 grams/6 oz/1½ cups
  flour, sifted with
  3 tspns baking powder.

Grease and line a 15 cm (6 inch) cake tin. Sift together the dry ingredients. Add the butter, eggs, vanilla essence and beat well. Add extra milk if required. Spoon into the prepared cake tin and bake at 180°C/350°F/Regulo 4 for 20-30 minutes or until soft and spongy. Turn out and allow to cool on a wire cake rack.
Slice the cake in half lengthwise and sandwich together with some of the Angel's Hair and whipped cream. Decorate the top with Angel's Hair.

Ginger Bread

I picked this recipe up from an old handwritten cookbook of the early 18th century. Second time around, I added 2 tspns of baking powder. The lack of punctuation is the lady herself's omission not mine!

"Take one Pound of Treakle 3 tspns ginger 1 tspn cinnamon 1 tspn mixed spice pinch salt and sift them then set your Treakle upon the Fire put in a pound of Sugar and break in a pound of Butter then put in all the spices and stir them well together until the Butter is all melted and then let it simmer and then take it off the Fire and let it stand till almost cold and put in Two pound and of Flour and make up into small Nuts and bake them on tin plates in a Quick Oven they are soon baked."

From the top left: Banana Cake, Angel's Hair Cake, Carrot Cake, New Style Fruit Cake.

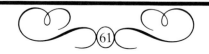

National Gallery

The great National Gallery of Ireland can be found in Merrion Square. It was built to the design of Francis Fowke in 1859 and opened five years later. It was conceived principally by William Dargan, a wealthy railway builder who was the driving force behind the Great Exhibition held in London in 1853. On display at the exhibition were a number of paintings and these later formed the nucleus of the collection now to be seen at the Gallery. In recognition of this, there is a statue of Dargan in the grounds.

Outside the entrance to the building stands another statue – that of the Irish playwright, George Bernard Shaw. It is due, in no small measure, to his generosity (he bequeathed a third of his estate to the Gallery) that the collection of paintings has grown to its present magnitude. It comprises a selection of the Irish School together with representative works from the French, Italian and Spanish Schools as well as works of the great Dutch masters.

The Main Staircase, The National Gallery.

JAMS AND PRESERVES

Apple & Ginger Conserve

5 oranges.
3 litres/5¼ pints/13 cups
   water.
1.350 kgs/3 lb apples.
2.5 kgs/5½ lb/11 cups jam
   sugar.

225 grams/8 oz/1½ cups
   glacé ginger.
15 grams/½ oz ground
   ginger.

Cut oranges in half and squeeze out all juice.
Cut the rind into pieces. Put in a pan with
the juice. Tie the pips and apple peel in a
muslin bag. Put into a pan with water and let
simmer for 1½-2 hours or until contents are
reduced by half. Discard the muslin bag. Cut
the apples into quarters, remove cores. Stew
over a low heat with about 120 ml/4 fl oz/½
cup of water. Mash well and add to the
oranges. Add the sugar, and glacé and ground
ginger. Boil for 10-15 minutes and test on a
plate. When set put into hot jars and cover.

Microwave Marmalade

This marmalade is not good for putting down.
However it is very quick and easy to make, so
make it as you need it.

500 grams/1 lb 2 oz
   oranges and lemons.
1 medium sized carrot.
680 grams/1½ lb/3 cups
   jam sugar.

350 ml/12 fl oz/1½ cups
   water.

Shred the oranges, lemons and carrot. (Cut
very fine). Place in a bowl with water. Put in
the microwave, bring to the boil, reduce
setting and cook for 10 minutes. Add the
sugar and stir well. Return to the microwave,
bring to the boil. Reduce the setting to
medium and cook for a further 20 minutes.
Pour into warm jars and seal.

Grape Conserve

900 grams/2 lb red
  grapes.
2 medium oranges.
250 ml/8 fl oz/1 cup
  water.
125 grams/5 oz/1 cup
  raisins.

570 grams/1¼ lb/2½ cups
  jam sugar.
110 grams/4 oz/1 cup
  walnuts, chopped.

Remove grapes from stems and cook the fruit in the water until tender. Squeeze juice from the oranges and cut the skins very finely. Cook the grape pulp, orange juice, peel and raisins until thick. Add sugar and boil gently for 15 minutes. Lastly add nuts and pour into clean, hot jars and seal.

Mint Jelly

1.350 kgs/3 lb green tart
  apples, unpeeled.
750 ml/1¼ pints/3 cups
  water.
Generous bunch of mint.
600 ml/1 pint/2½ cups
  malt vinegar.

Jam
Sugar
5 tblspns extra chopped
  mint.

Wash the apples. Quarter and place in a pan with the water and the bunch of mint (well washed). Simmer until the apples are soft and reduced to a pulp. Add vinegar and cook for a further five minutes. Put into a muslin bag and let drip overnight.
Next day: Measure extract and return to pan with 450 grams/1 lb/2 cups of sugar to every 600 ml/1 pint/2½ cups extract. Boil rapidly until setting point is reached. Stir in the extra chopped mint.
Pour into warm jars. Cover and seal.

BRAM STOKER
1847 – 1912
THEATRE MANAGER
AUTHOR OF DRACULA
LIVED HERE

Dublin Castle

Dublin Castle, partially hidden in a cluster of rather ugly office blocks, presents an Irish anachronism – a vice-regal past in a staunchly republican present.

Of all the buildings in Dublin it most awesomely reflects the City's turbulent and often bloody past yet inside it is the most beautifully gentle of buildings with colour and pattern and antiquity woven together to form an inspiring whole. The Millenium year saw many millions of pounds spent on the building to host the European Parliament in the early 1990's.

The original Castle was built in 1204 but little of the original is left, although important remnants of the medieval period have survived. In the 18th century a very commanding castle complex seems to have stood on the site which was then the administrative, social and cultural centre of Dublin.

Today the most notable remains are the splendid state apartments, some redecorated after a fire in 1941.

Over the inner gate stands the Statue of Justice. She has always faced into the courtyard and 18th century cynics claimed that Justice had turned her back on Dublin. From time to time her scales would hang unevenly as rain water collected in different amounts in each pan (her outstretched arm sheltered one) - which led the over-sensitive Castle authorities to bore holes in the pans to let the water out!

For well they laughed with counterfeited glee at all his jokes, for many a joke had he.

> *The village schoolmaster in "The Deserted Village" by Oliver Goldsmith, 1730-1774.*

The State Apartments, Dublin Castle.

COFFEE

Irish Coffee

1) Take a stemmed glass.
2) Put in 2 teaspoonfuls of sugar.
3) Add a measure of Irish Whiskey – the essential ingredient for traditional Irish Coffee – and stir.
4) Pour in hot, strong coffee to within 1¼ cm (½ inch) of the rim.

5) Finally, float on a collar of lightly whipped cream.
DO NOT STIR.
6) Sip the hot coffee and Irish Whiskey through the cool cream to gain an unrivalled taste sensation.

SIR
WILLIAM
ROBERT WILLS
WILDE, 1815 – 1876,
aural and ophthalmic
surgeon, archaeologist,
ethnologist, antiquarian,
biographer, statistician,
naturalist, topographer,
historian, folklorist,
lived in this house
from 1855 to 1876

Irish Coffee

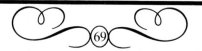

The Whiskey Corner

"The Whiskey Corner" is an interesting museum of Irish Whiskey tracing its history back to medieval times.

Over 1000 years ago when missionary monks brought the art of distilling to Ireland, they used the technique to distill alcohol for perfume, but the Irish soon found a better use for it – to make "Uisce Beatha" (meaning "water of life") later anglicised to "Fuisce" which finally became whiskey. As distinct from its Scottish counterpart, Irish Whiskey is spelt "ey".

The famous companies included John Jameson, Old Bushmills, Black Bush, Powers, Paddy, Crested Ten, Murphy's and Tullamore Dew with it's famous slogan – "Give every man his Dew".

Amongst the famous partial to Irish Whiskey were Sir Walter Raleigh who stopped in Co. Cork to collect a 32 gallon cask before embarking on his epic voyages to America, Queen Elizabeth I favoured the drink and Czar Peter the Great proclaimed that "of all the wines, the Irish spirit is the best". Today Irish Whiskey is still made in much the same way as it was when, around 1380 Sir Robert Savage fortified his troops before battle with "a mighty draft".

The Whiskey Corner.

Rotunda Hospital

At the northern end of O'Connell Street in Parnell Square stands the first, purpose-built maternity hospital in the British Isles – the Rotunda. Unusually ornate for such a building, it was the brainchild of one Dr Mosse, an Irish barber surgeon who had been impressed by a visit to the famous teaching hospital, the Hotel Dieu in Paris.

The building commenced in 1751, to the design of Richard Cassels (sometimes called Castle) a German architect who had settled in Ireland some 25 years earlier.

The copper dome which dominates the building and which has been criticised as an unnecessary extravagance in a hospital, was added in the hope that it might be utilised as an astronomical observatory – and so raise money for the hospital.

The observatory never materialised but the grounds which were turned into public gardens, did achieve this objective. The chapel above the entrance hall was completed in 1778 and has impressive plasterwork by Bartholomew Crimillion. The interior is quite beautiful and is one of Dublin's most spectacular artistic treasures.

Today the Rotunda is still a leading teaching hospital, with more than two centuries of tradition and prestige behind it.

OLIVER ST. JOHN GOGARTY
POET AND SURGEON
HAD ROOMS HERE
1915 – 1917

Rotunda Hospital Chapel

The Shelbourne Hotel

When does a hotel become a legend? Ask the Shelbourne. If you want to stay at the most distinguished hotel address in the city, sign a constitution or just rub shoulders with all the best people, then Dubliners will say "the Shelbourne it must be" – and who am I to disagree? William Makepeace Thackeray would never have dreamed of staying anywhere else. It stands in dignified hauteur, early Victoriana in a Dublin Georgian enclave. Outside, its Nubian Princesses and their slaves on stone pedestals face St. Stephen's Green while in front of them, on the pavement, an incongruous paper-seller plies his trade with the morning and evening editions.

The hotel opened its doors in November of 1824 when Martin Burke bought No's 27, 28 and 29 St. Stephen's Green for the sum of £3,000 and a rent of £300 per year. (He later bought No's 30 and 31).

The hotel was renamed after William, second Earl of Shelbourne. In 1863 the hotel was sold to William Jury (founder of Jury's Hotel) Charles Cotten, owner of The Imperial Hotel, Cork and Christian Goodman who managed The Railway Hotel, Killarney.

In 1867 it was knocked down and rebuilt on a finer and much grander scale with sophisticated additions such as a coffee room, a telegraph room, a hairdressing salon and a general reading room. In the Constitution Room on the first floor Darrell Figgus and his colleagues met in 1922 to draw up the Irish Constitution.

The sumptuous front bedrooms have an aerial view of the park, the ducks on the pond and the splendid gardens. Inside and out, marble and brass shine with a glow produced by decades of polish and elbow grease. This hotel with its grand and noble aura, is inextricably woven into Dublin's history. Dine in the Aisling Restaurant, have a Guinness or a Jameson's in the Horseshoe Bar, or a traditional afternoon tea in the Lord Mayor's Lounge – it could be one of your tour's great indulgences.

Exterior of The Shelbourne Hotel

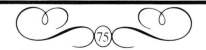

St. Stephen's Green

Undoubtedly one of the pleasantest places in Dublin is the 24 acres of St Stephen's Green – a great enclosed park with formal gardens, a man-made lake, green lawns, shady trees and a sizeable population of statues, ducks and birds. It was a "common" in medieval times and was enclosed in 1663. The Guinness brewer, Lord Ardilaun laid it out in its present form and opened it as a public park in 1880. His seated statue faces in the direction of his brewery in St James's Gate. Other statues include James Joyce looking towards his old alma mater, University College opposite. At the South East corner, three bronze female figures over a fountain were a gift from the West German people in appreciation of Ireland's help after World War II.

Elsewhere in the park are statues of Wolfe Tone and Jeremiah O'Donovan Rossa, both Irish separatist heroes, and W.B. Yeats – poet and more. A nice touch, which reflects the gentle side of the Irish character is a small garden for blind children with more robust flowers which can be handled, and with identification tags in braille. Untouched by developers over its long history, the park has ducks that float, flowers that bloom, fountains that fount and birds that sing very happily indeed.

FAILTE DUBHLINN

ENGINEER
GEOLOGIST VALUATOR
SIR RICHARD GRIFFITH
1784 – 1878

LIVED HERE 1828 – 1878

Entrance to St. Stephen's Green.

University Church

Leaving the south side of the "Green" from
Grafton Street, past the bespectacled James
Joyce, brings you face to face with the Neo-
Byzantine University Church. Cardinal
Newman brought John Hungerford Pollen
from England to design the collegiate church
and it was built between 1854 and 1856.
Inside, it has been lavishly and extensively
decorated with marble brought from all over
Ireland. It is a very beautiful church,
fashionable for weddings.

University Church.

Modern Dublin

Within the Grafton Street area are some of Dublin's most sophisticated shops – in the new Hibernian Arcade, the stunning Powerscourt Centre, and Nassau Street, which runs parallel to the railings south of Trinity College.

There are colonades, laneways and acres of shopping space in wall-to-wall expensive good taste. Weirs, Brown Thomas, Switzer's, the Kilkenny Shop and Blarney Woollen Mills, all come to mind.

This part of Dublin changes almost daily and one wonders if there isn't some little leprechaun in the City Hall continually planning how to pull it all apart and then how to put all back together again!

After a good dinner one can forgive anybody,
even one's own relatives.
        (Oscar Wilde, 1856-1900)

Modern Dublin, Grafton Street.

Guinness Steak and Kidney

225 grams/8 oz stewing steak, (cut into 1¼ cm/ ½ inch cubes).
2 lambs kidneys (skinned, cored and cut into small pieces).
1 medium sized onion (finely chopped).
150 ml/¼ pint/⅝ cup beef stock.
½ tspn Worcestershire Sauce.
4-5 tblspns Guinness.
55 grams/2 oz mushrooms (finely sliced).
Salt & pepper.
1 tspn cornflour.
Chopped parsley.

Heat 1-2 tblspns oil in a saucepan. Add the meat, kidney, onion and brown well. Add beef stock, Worcestershire Sauce and Guinness. Cover and simmer gently for about 1 hour until meat is tender. Add mushrooms and seasoning, cook for a further 15 minutes. Remove a little of the stock and blend with the cornflour. Return to steak and kidney. Bring to boil, stir and cook for 1-2 minutes. Sprinkle with chopped parsley and serve. SERVES 2.

From left to right, Guinness Steak and Kidney, Guinness Cake and Guinness Christmas Pudding.

Index

Dips n' Dunks	6
Fruit & Nut Dip	6
Apricot & Cottage Cheese Dip	6
Avocado Dip	7
Garden Dip	7
Soups	11
Cucumber Soup	11
Potato and Chervil Soup	11
Onion Soup with White Wine	12
Breads, Muffins & Butters	15
Date & Bran Tea-Loaf	15
Aussie Damper	15
Barmbrack	16
Shelbourne Hotel Brown Bread	16
Irish Wholemeal Soda Bread	17
Herb Soda Bread	17
Cornmeal Bread	18
White Soda Bread	18
Muffins	19
Cornmeal Muffins	19
Muesli Muffins	19
Raspberry Muffins	20
Orange Muffins	20

Savoury Butters	21
Grain Mustard Butter	21
Red Paprika Butter	21
Garlic Butter	21
Herb Butter	21
Salads	25
Capsicum and Kiwifruit Salad	25
Celery and Apple Salad	25
Coleslaw with Toasted Hazlenuts	26
Cucumber in Sour Cream Sauce	26
Fish	29
Cockle and Mussel Medley with Garlic Dressing	29
Crab with Mango with Avocado served with Lemon Dressing	29
Dublin Bay Grilled Prawns	30
Fillets of Sole St. Brigid	30
Smoked Salmon Roulade	31
Whole Salmon in Red Wine	31
Seafood Strudel with Pepper and Chives Sauce	32
Whole Plaice with Grapes	32
Fillo Envelopes	33
Sea Trout Strudel with Hot Tartare Sauce	33
Parfait of Seafood with Avocado Sauce	34

Index

Main Courses	**37**
Chicken with Mangoes	37
Cold Chicken with Yoghurt, Herbs and Kiwifruit Mayonnaise	37
Lamb Cutlets with Pineapple, Barbecue Style	38
Rack of Wicklow Lamb with Honey and Herbs	38
Pork Fillets and Avocado with Cheese Sauce	39
Loin of Pork, with Honey Glaze	39
Guinness Steak and Kidney	83

Vegetables	**43**
Baked Onions with Walnuts	43
Colcannon	43
Hot Potato Salad	44
Garlic Parsnips in Sour Cream	44

Desserts	**47**
Lemon Cups	47
Guinness Christmas Pudding	47
Gateau Emo	48
Downunder Christmas Pudding	48
Cream Cheese Slice	49
Raisin Pie	49

Fruit Salads	**53**
Fruit Salad with Toasted Almonds	53
Winter Fruit Salad	53
Berry Salad	54
Melon Salad with Brandy and Wine	54
Grapefruit St. Patrick	54
Hot Banana and Orange Salad	55
Tutti Frutti	55

Cakes	**59**
New Style Fruit Cake	59
Guinness Cake	59
Banana Cake	60
Carrot Cake	60
Angel's Hair Cake	61
Ginger Bread	61

Jams & Preserves	**65**
Apple & Ginger Conserve	65
Microwave Marmalade	65
Grape Conserve	66
Mint Jelly	66

Coffee	**69**
Irish Coffee	69

The End

I wish to express my indebtedness to the various establishments for their recipes as well as friends and colleagues who have given me both their time and assistance to produce the material for this book.

Gillian Berwick

It isn't so much what's on the table that matters
as what's on the chairs.
W.S. Gilbert, 1836-1911,
(of Gilbert & Sullivan fame)

College Green

89